ARRESTED FOR DUI IN SOUTHERN CALIFORNIA?

(Revealed: Useful Info That May Help You Fight Your Charges)

By Manuel J. Barba, DUI Defense Attorney

ISBN: 978-1-941645-08-6

Design and Published by:

Speakeasy Marketing, Inc.
73-03 Bell Blvd #10
Oakland Gardens, NY11364

www.SpeakeasyMarketingInc.com

DISCLAIMER

This publication is informational only. No legal advice is being given, and reading this material creates no attorney-client relationship. If you are facing legal issues, whether criminal or civil, seek professional legal counsel to have your questions answered.

Law Office of Manuel J. Barba
3800 Orange Street, Suite 100
Riverside, CA 92501
(866) 442-2722 | (951) 680-9125 | (760) 770-3377

www.BarbaLawyer.com
www.aggressiveDUIdefense.com
www.PalmSpringsDUI.com

Peer Endorsements

"Mr. Barba is one of the new breeds of lawyers known as the lawyer-scientist. When defending a person accused of driving under the influence it is imperative that the lawyer have a deep understanding of the science behind blood and breath testing. Very few lawyers spend the time necessary to be a lawyer-scientist. Mr. Barba has and does. You are in good hands with Mr. Barba representing you on an alcohol related charge.

-Josh Lee, DUI / DWI Attorney in Vinita, OK

"Attorney Barba is an experienced trial advocate. He has the necessary reputation, knowledge, experience and guts needed to defend those accused of a crime. He has earned a national reputation for his years of successful advocacy. Most of all, I trust him. I know you will too."

-Justin McShane, DUI / DWI Attorney in Harrisburg, PA

"I highly recommend Mr. Barba. Not only was he one of my Standardized Field Sobriety Test course instructors but he is also extremely knowledgeable on all DUI matters. He has also proven to be a skilled and successful trial attorney."

-Mark Rosenfeld, DUI / DWI Attorney in Beverly Hills, CA

"I have watched this attorney masterfully defend his clients throughout Riverside County. I would highly recommend him on DUI's. He has the knowledge, the ability and the drive to get his clients great results. He is an asset to the legal community."

-Melanie Roe, Criminal Defense Atty., Rancho Mirage, CA

Client Testimonials

"I live in Los Angeles and I was arrested in Riverside County for suspected DUI, while on vacation. Mr. Barba and his team of professionals fought for me in court through all of the hearings and trial. I don't believe another attorney could have fought for me any harder against the D.A. and the highway patrol. I saw his experience in DUI trials first hand. He was able to present an outstanding case and subsequently got a "Not Guilty" verdict on my behalf. If you are being accused of a DUI, I strongly suggest you hire an attorney who specializes in DUI cases like Mr. Barba."

– Robert

....

"Manny Barba and his staff were both extremely knowledgeable and informative from the first day they took my case. Taken as a referral from a close friend, Mr. Barba not only exceeded my legal expectations, but gave my family and me an additional feeling of wellbeing throughout the process." ***– Johnny***

....

"Mr. Barba is an excellent attorney who has extensive knowledge in his area of expertise. I am glad I hired him and would recommend him to others in DUI defense. I was facing a second conviction and it was reduced to a wet reckless, this saved my career." ***– Michael***

....

"Mr. Barba is a phenomenal attorney and he knows everything about how to defend a DUI. And believe me you will get that impression when you see him in action - that he is an expert and everyone else is a novice. To my friends or anyone that is in need of a DUI defense team. DO NOT THINK TWICE!! Call Mr. Barba's office. You want him in your corner." ***-Adesan***

TABLE OF CONTENTS

Attorney Introduction

Southern California DUI Defense Attorney Manuel J. Barba is an expert in DUI Defense and is dedicated to defending people accused of DUI, as well as other driving related cases.

Attorney Manuel J. Barba represents people accused of DUI throughout Riverside County, San Bernardino County, Imperial County, Orange County, and Los Angeles County.

DUI Defense Attorney Manuel J. Barba has been awarded the AV® Preeminent™ rating from Martindale-Hubbell®. For more than 130 years, lawyers have relied on the AV® Preeminent™ rating while searching for their own expert attorneys. Now anyone can depend on this important, trusted rating. The Martindale-Hubbell® AV® Preeminent™ rating is the highest possible rating for an attorney for both ethical standards and legal ability. This rating represents the pinnacle of professional excellence. It is achieved only after an attorney has been reviewed and recommended by their peers - members of the bar and the judiciary.

In addition, Attorney Manuel J. Barba has been awarded a "superb 10 rating" by Avvo.com, the highest rating a lawyer can receive.

DUI Attorney Manuel J. Barba is a Specialist member of the California DUI Lawyers Association and is a member of its Board of Directors. Attorney Barba is also an active member of the National College for DUI Defense, California Attorneys for Criminal Justice, California Public Defenders Association, and the National Association of Criminal Defense Lawyers. Attorney Manuel J. Barba has also attended the National Criminal Defense College in Macon, Georgia, as well as the Trial Lawyers College in Dubois, Wyoming.

Attorney Manuel J. Barba is also a nationally recognized Standardized Field Sobriety Test Instructor, having completed the National Highway Traffic Safety Administration (NHTSA) / International Association of Chiefs of Police (IACP) DWI Detection Standardized Field Sobriety Testing Instructor Program, and has taught SFST courses throughout the United States to other lawyers.

Attorney Barba is also trained in Advanced Roadside Impaired Driving Enforcement (ARIDE) program in addition to Drug Recognition Expert (DRE) protocols, both developed by the National Highway Traffic Safety Administration (NHTSA) and the International Association of Chiefs of Police (IACP), which gives attorney Barba the specialized knowledge necessary to evaluate arrests made by law enforcement officers for DUI-Drugs and skillfully cross-examine the arresting officer on issues related to drug evaluation protocols.

In addition, attorney Manuel J. Barba has received advanced training in Forensic Blood and Urine Analysis as it relates to testing for Alcohol and Drugs, including advanced courses in Gas Chromatography and Mass Spectrometry at Axion Analytical Laboratories, Inc. in Chicago, taught by Dr. Harold McNair and Dr. Lee Polite. Gas Chromatography and Mass Spectrometry are the processes generally used to analyze blood and urine samples for alcohol and drug content.

Attorney Manuel J. Barba is also an expert in Breath Testing Analysis, having attended various advanced courses related to breath alcohol testing analysis.

Attorney Barba is also a member of the American Chemical Society (ACS), which is the world's largest scientific society and one of the world's leading sources of authoritative scientific information. A nonprofit organization, chartered by Congress, ACS is at the forefront of the evolving worldwide chemical enterprise and the premier professional home for chemists, chemical engineers and related professions around the globe.

Attorney Barba was also awarded the "Top Lawyers" award by Palm Springs Life Magazine and Inland Empire Magazine in both 2012 and 2013.

A DUI Defense Attorney Helps to Protect the Rights of Individuals

Interviewer: How did you become a DUI Defense Attorney and why?

Manuel Barba: I have always found DUI Defense to be very interesting in the sense that it deals with protecting people's rights and protecting people from the government. Many people are arrested for DUI and some of them are truly not guilty.

In my career as a lawyer, I've seen a lot of overreaching by the government including: prosecutors, cops, crime lab personnel, etc. They try to corner people. They try to manipulate the facts and evidence. They have predetermined assumptions about particular things. They are not always being objective and they are not always trying to give people a fair shake. They are trying to get a conviction. People who have been arrested for DUI need to be protected; they need to have an attorney that is a *scientist-lawyer* and is an expert in DUI Defense. It's not enough to know the law; the attorney has to know the science as well.

DUI Defense Is Science-Based

The more DUI cases that I handled, the more I found them very fascinating because they are very scientific in nature. Basically, there is an officer that stops a driver for some vehicle code violation (speeding, etc.) and just happens to smell alcohol, then asks the driver if he/she has been drinking, and then wants the driver to exit the car and perform some kind of field sobriety tests, "standardized" or otherwise (what I call roadside gymnastics).

Well, how accurate are these tests and what, if anything, do they mean? Things like this interest me so I studied field sobriety tests, from their development including the studies claiming to validate these tests, as well as the independent studies that show that these tests are designed to fail.

"It is actually NOT Illegal to Drink and Drive in California—it is Illegal to drive a Vehicle if you are "Under the Influence" of an Impairing Substance."

In studying these field sobriety tests, as well as the science behind chemical tests, I've learned that people arrested for DUI aren't always impaired, nor are the chemical test results always accurate.

In California, it's not illegal to drink and drive. It's only illegal if at the time of driving the driver is "under the influence" of a substance, whether it is alcohol or a drug (VC23152 (a) (e)). Being "under the influence" is a factual conclusion that has to be proved with evidence that is *reliable,* and *beyond reasonable doubt* (this is the prosecutor's burden of proof).

It is also illegal to *drive* with a blood alcohol concentration (BAC) that is 0.08% or higher (VC23152 (b)), which is another conclusion that must be proved by the government with evidence that is *reliable,* and *beyond reasonable doubt (*this too is the prosecutor's burden).

Sometimes the government cannot meet their burden, meaning the prosecutor can't prove *beyond a reasonable doubt* that the driver was "under the influence" or was "driving with a BAC that is 0.08% or higher "because when you analyze all of the evidence, you find that the government's conclusions are wrong, or there are multiple interpretations of the evidence, and therefore the accused person really is not guilty.

Remember, the fact that a person consumed alcohol doesn't mean that the person is *impaired* by the alcohol!

Determining a Driver's Blood Alcohol Level

Blood alcohol testing is an attempt by law enforcement to determine how much alcohol is in a driver's bloodstream. If a blood alcohol test result is 0.08% or higher, a driver is *presumed* to have violated the law (Vehicle Code 23152(b)). Keep in mind that the defense can present evidence, either through cross examination or affirmatively, that the test result is unreliable.

It is important to remember that the blood alcohol test is supposed to determine the driver's blood alcohol concentration ***at the time of driving the car,*** and not after the fact. There can be a significant difference between a driver's blood alcohol concentration at the time of driving and the time the test is taken, which sometimes occurs an hour or more later.

The two most common tests that a law enforcement officer uses to determine a person's blood alcohol concentration is a breath test, where the driver blows into a device; and the blood test, where the driver's blood is drawn for analysis.

Various factors such as gender, the amount of alcohol consumed, the person's weight, the type of alcohol that was consumed, the time of consumption, and any food consumption, can directly impact the reliability of the results of these tests.

Breath Alcohol Testing

During a breath test the person blows into a breath analysis device. Although there is a relationship (known as the ***partition ratio)*** between a person's breath alcohol and the alcohol concentration in the person's blood, this relationship varies by a number of factors and is *not* constant. The "science" of breath alcohol testing assumes that the relationship, or partition ratio, between a person's breath and blood is always the same for all people and at all times. However, in reality, that relationship varies widely, thus often making breath alcohol testing results unreliable.

In addition, the science of breath alcohol testing **assumes** that the subject has ***fully absorbed*** all of the alcohol that the person drank, which means that all of the alcohol the person drank is no longer in their stomach or small intestine - all of the alcohol has been absorbed into the blood stream and the alcohol has reached ***equilibrium*** throughout the person's body. This means that the alcohol concentration is the same throughout the body, so if a blood sample was taken from a person's ear lobe, and another blood sample was taken from the person's toe, and both samples were analyzed for alcohol content, the alcohol concentration would be essentially the same.

If a person has NOT fully absorbed the alcohol that they drank, then the breath testing result will not be reliable because the assumption of full absorption has not been met, and the breath testing device will overstate the results by 2 to 3 times, as shown in a number of scientific studies.

Scientific studies show that it can take as much as two to six hours to absorb all of the alcohol that a person drank, depending on when the person last ate in relation to drinking, what they ate, what they drank, etc. Thus, if a person drank 2 or 3 drinks with dinner, then was driving home, and then was stopped by an officer on his/her way home and blew into a breath machine; the breath machine might show a result of .12 - .14 BAC, when in reality the person's actual blood alcohol concentration is .04 to .06.

The reality is most persons don't know if they are still absorbing the alcohol that they drank, especially if they were eating, thus they should NEVER agree to blow into a breath testing device. Always request a blood test and blow into nothing.

Blood Alcohol Testing

A person's blood alcohol content can be determined by testing a sample of the person's blood. Compared to a breath test, a blood test is generally a more accurate method to determine a person's blood alcohol concentration if the analysis is done correctly. However, blood alcohol analysis is a very complicated process and there are many factors related to blood testing that can cause the result to be unreliable.

During a blood alcohol test, blood is drawn from a person's vein, usually from the arm, and then it is eventually analyzed using a very complicated process known as gas chromatography. If the blood test reveals the person's blood alcohol concentration to be 0.08% or greater, that person is considered to be in violation of law (VC23152 (b)). The question is: **Is the blood test result reliable?**

The reliability of the blood test result is often an issue in the defense of a DUI case due to a number of factors including contamination of the blood sample itself during handling and storage of the sample, as well as the accuracy and reliability of the gas chromatography process.

To the untrained observer, the blood test result itself might be the end of the analysis. Many lawyers that pretend to defend persons accused of DUI will look at the blood test result and say: "*Yep, your blood test result is a 0.16%...that's twice the legal limit; we better plead you guilty because nothing can be done to defend your case.*"

Even most prosecutors simply rely on the blood test result believing that the result is infallible, when in reality they know nothing about how the crime lab got to the result.

Remember back in math class in high school or college? If you turned your homework in with nothing but a list of answers, would you get a good grade on your homework? NO! Why? Because your math teacher wanted you to show your work; the teacher wanted to see HOW you got the answer!

The same is true with blood testing, which is a scientific process. To know whether the result is accurate and reliable, the crime lab needs to show their work as to how they arrived at the result.

I have said to many jurors: "*You have to be the math teacher and require the government to prove that the blood test result is accurate and reliable; the government has to show you their work."*

The first question with any blood test analysis is: **How was the blood sample analysis performed?** Meaning what type of method was used. Was the analysis completed using an Enzyme Assay test? Was the analysis done by Gas Chromatography (GC)? If Gas Chromatography was used, then what type of *separation* equipment was used as part of the process? If GC was used, then what type of *analysis* equipment was used as part of the process? The answers to all of these questions are very important as there are a number of potential problems associated with each method.

As one can see from the previous discussion, *science* plays a significant role in the proper defense of a DUI case.

When defending a person accused of driving under the influence it is imperative that the lawyer has a deep understanding of the science behind blood alcohol testing and breath testing. Unfortunately, very few lawyers spend the time necessary to become a lawyer-scientist, and their clients suffer as a result. You cannot defend a DUI case if you do not know the science involved.

Is DUI Prosecution Influenced by Politics?

Interviewer: Why do television and the media in general refer to Driving Under the Influence (DUI) as "Drunk Driving?" Why does the government create the impression that drunk drivers are out on the streets killing people in great numbers?

Manuel Barba: That becomes the political aspect of DUI, because it really is a political crime. There is a certain group of people, whether they are members of law enforcement or other government players, Mothers Against Drunk Driving (MADD), etc., that in essence want to see prohibition again, where it is illegal to drink alcohol, period.

The reality is, even during prohibition in the United States (1920–1933) it was not illegal to drink alcohol. It was only illegal under federal law to manufacture, transport, and sell alcohol. The events that led up to prohibition are an interesting read. The bottom line is the prohibition of alcohol was a failure as it lead to organized crime and other problems. Nevertheless, there are those today with the agenda to outlaw alcohol.

Now I am not saying that excessive consumption of alcohol and driving is a good thing – it is not. People are needlessly killed on the roadways by drunk drivers, but it doesn't happen as much as the government would like you to believe. The government's statistics are not completely honest, but that's the subject of another book.

The point is, many persons arrested for DUI are not "drunk drivers" and are not "impaired." Most persons arrested for DUI went out to dinner and had a couple drinks (beer, wine, etc.), and then on their way home from the restaurant they are stopped by a cop for some basic driving error (i.e., speed, rolling a stop sign, not using turn signal, etc.) and it goes downhill from there. Wanting to cooperate, the unsuspecting citizen admits to the cop that they drank a glass or two of wine with dinner. The cop then has the person perform field sobriety tests that are designed to fail. Then the cop may have the person blow into a preliminary alcohol screen device, which will overstate the results because the person just finished drinking. Then the person is arrested for DUI.

What the public doesn't realize is that law enforcement agencies get grant money for every DUI arrest they make (it's practically a bounty) and it has become a mechanism for funding. For every DUI conviction, the courts, the DMV, the crime lab, and the law enforcement agency all get cut of the fine paid to the court. All of these governmental agencies have a vested interest in seeing that the accused person is convicted. The politics are that DUI arrests and convictions are money makers for the state agencies.

The Government Encourages the Prosecution of Drug-Related DUIs and these Numbers Continue to Grow

Interviewer: What are the main types of DUI cases you've handled? Do you deal with drug related DUI cases?

Manuel Barba: DUIs are not just alcohol. The big push today by the government is DUI drugs. When I say drugs, I don't just mean cocaine, heroin, marijuana, or some other illegal drug. The government is starting to go after people for driving after taking prescription medications claiming that these medications impair driving. Seriously, the government is trying to convict people because of the prescription medication that they are taking. I see a number of cases involving prescribed pain killers, anxiety medications, muscle relaxers, sleeping aids, you name it!

The government wants to expand the definition of DUI drivers well beyond alcohol. I have clients with these types of cases. To the government, it's all about making more money.

People are shocked when they find out that they can be arrested for DUI for driving after taking their prescribed medication.

How does it happen? A person is stopped for some vehicle code violation (i.e., speed, rolling a stop sign, not using turn signal, etc.) and again, it goes downhill from there. The officer asks the driver if they've been drinking, and when the driver says NO, the officer asks "are you taking any medications?" Again, wanting to cooperate, the unsuspecting citizen admits to the cop that he/she took their [prescribed medication] an hour ago "like I do every day. "The cop then has the person exit the car, performs the field sobriety tests that are designed to fail. Then the cop then arrests the person for driving under the influence of [prescribed medication] which is a violation of VC23152 (e). Thereafter a sample of the person's blood is drawn, analyzed, and the crime lab finds the metabolites of the medication. The prosecutor then files charges and tries to convict the person for DUI. And having a prescription is not necessarily a defense.

It really is a racket by the government to make more money and convict more people of crimes. Again, it's the politics of funding the governmental agencies.

Pseudo-Science and Errors in Methods of Analysis Lead to Inaccurate Results

Because of the politics geared towards convicting people accused of DUI, governmental agencies (including crime labs) have created their own version of science; it is junk science or pseudoscience.

"Pseudoscience "is a claim, belief or practice which is presented as *scientific*, but does not adhere to a valid scientific, lacks supporting evidence or plausibility, cannot be reliably tested, or otherwise lacks scientific status.

Here's how the government charade works as far as DUI prosecution is concerned. Law enforcement creates its own system of crime labs and pseudo scientists that they refer to as "criminalists." They even create their own state organizations to give them credibility. The criminalist's job is to conduct forensic analysis of blood and urine samples to get results that will support a conviction of the accused person. Criminalists also maintain the breath testing machines.

Then when an accused citizen goes to trial on their DUI case, the criminalist, who is a member of the law enforcement team, comes to court as a witness for the prosecution to testify that the test results are correct, that the machine was working properly, and that the person operating the machine was properly trained.

The problem is that most of these criminalists know very little about the real scientific concepts and theories related to the issues that they are testifying about. They usually testify in court that they have reviewed "*the scientific literature*" related to a particular subject, but on cross- examination they can never remember the title of even one relevant scientific paper that has been peer reviewed.

Often times, when pressed on a particular issue during cross-examination, the criminalist's lack of true scientific knowledge becomes evident to the jury.

This is why it is imperative that a lawyer defending a DUI case must have a deep understanding of the science behind blood alcohol testing and breath testing. The DUI defense lawyer must know the science better than the state criminalist and better than the prosecution.

In California, a DUI Conviction Is "Priorable" for a 10-Year Period

Interviewer: Have you worked with people who have had multiple DUIs?

Manuel Barba: I've worked with many people that have had multiple DUIs. In California, a DUI offense is "priorable" for 10 years. This means that if a person gets a DUI, the government looks back 10 years from the date of the current DUI violation to see if there are any prior DUI convictions. If so, the government will allege the prior convictions and the penalties will increase because of the prior conviction(s).

I have had many a client say "I will never do this again" but they come back to see me five or six years later with a new DUI. Ten years is a long time.

Rarely did anything serious happen. The person had a few beers with lunch, etc., and is stopped for some minor vehicle code violation, and the next thing you know, they are arrested for another DUI.

It's not hard to get a DUI, especially when law enforcement officers are out there looking for them. Remember, law enforcement agencies get grant money for every arrest they make. So cops are out looking for DUIs because they are a money maker for the state.

Geographic Areas Where I Practice

Interviewer: What counties or areas do you take handle DUI cases for clients?

Manuel Barba: I basically serve the Southern California area: Riverside County, San Bernardino County, Orange County, Los Angeles County, and Imperial County.

My main office is based in Riverside, California, and I have an office in the Palm Springs area, which is in the Coachella Valley area.

Is a Particular Demographic of the Population More Likely to Receive a DUI?

Manuel Barba: In my experience, the answer to that is NO. There's no typical person that receives a DUI.

I've represented older persons, sweet ladies that were out having dinner with friends and had a glass of wine. I've represented many young people who were out having beers, watching the game.

I have represented persons from all walks of life. I've represented doctors, nurses, teachers, firemen, police detectives, students, lawyers, truck drivers, paramedics, etc.

There is not any particular one type of person over another that gets arrested for DUI.

Fact or Fiction: Do Most People that Get Arrested for DUI Have High Blood Alcohol Levels?

Interviewer: The public seems to think or has been told, that people are drunk when they are arrested. Of the clients you see, do most of them have high blood alcohol levels? Are they close to the legal limit?

Most Individuals That Receive a DUI Have Lower Blood Alcohol Levels

Manuel Barba: Most of the people arrested for DUI have alleged blood alcohol concentrations (BAC) in the lower numbers. There are some that are higher in BAC, but the question becomes, is the higher number reliable? There are a number of reasons that a test result can show a high BAC but the number is inaccurate; this problem arises in both breath and blood testing. The low BAC number could be inaccurate as well.

Most people that get a DUI are just people that had a couple beers with dinner or a couple drinks during happy hour.

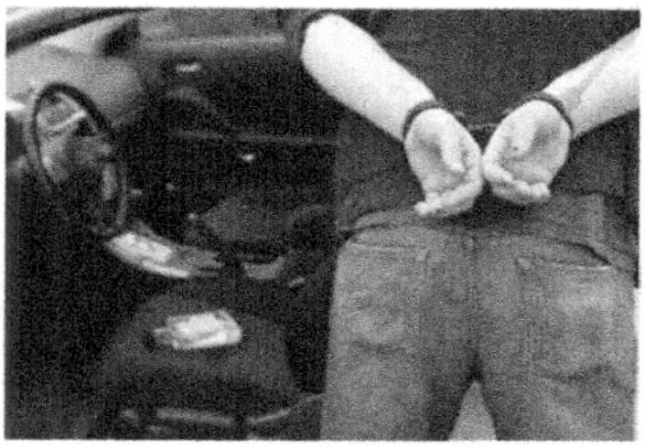

We're not talking about hardcore alcoholics. Law enforcement officers like to paint the picture that the people they arrest are impaired so they tend to embellish what is written in the arrest report.

Most people that get a DUI, just finished drinking and they unfortunately blew into a preliminary breath testing device; the breath machine will always overstate the results if the person is still absorbing the alcohol. Cops always claim that person failed the field sobriety tests no matter how well the person did.

ARE DUI ARRESTS GOOD BUSINESS FOR THE STATE GOVERNMENTS?

Interviewer: How many DUI arrests do you estimate there are in Southern California each year?

Manuel Barba: From the latest DMV statistics I have read, there were just over 180,000 DUI arrests in 2011 statewide.

For Riverside County there were approximately 10,000 DUI arrests in 2011; San Bernardino County there were almost 12,000 DUI arrests in 2011; Orange County there were just over 16,000 DUI arrests in 2011; and Los Angeles County there were just over 40,200 arrests in 2011.

Many Government Agencies Receive a Portion of the Fines Paid by Drivers Convicted of DUIs

There is an incentive to convict people of DUIs, because when somebody has to pay fines on a DUI conviction, the court gets part of that fine money. The crime lab that analyzes the blood gets part of that. The law enforcement agency gets part of that. The DMV gets part of that. Everybody has a vested interest in convicting people for DUIs. The public really doesn't know that.

Common Misconceptions about DUI Arrests

Interviewer: What are the top misconceptions your clients have about being arrested for DUI?

Exercise Your Fifth Amendment Right

Manuel Barba: Probably the biggest misconception that people have is that they have to do everything that the officer tells them to do. I think part of it is because people inherently want to cooperate with the officer. The person thinks "I didn't do anything wrong. I'm not drunk."

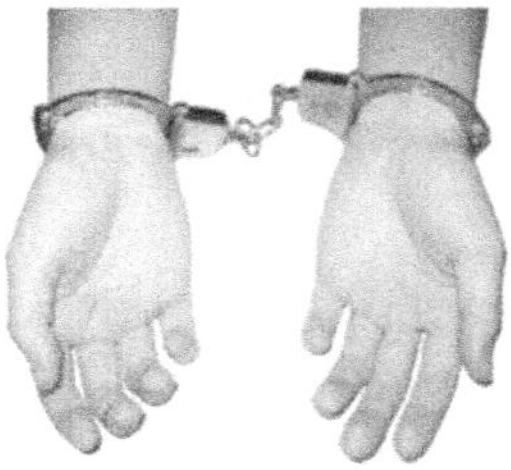

Even though all citizens have a Fifth Amendment (U.S. Constitution) right to remain silent and not answer questions that would incriminate them, people still answer the officer's questions! Did you drink? YES. What did you drink? Three beers. When did you drink? Etc.

All of these questions are incriminating and persons should not answer them and always remain silent. It is their right to do so. The person thinks "I'm going to do everything that the officer asks me to do and he will let me go...Right?" Wrong! If the officer smells alcohol he can arrest you just based on the odor.

It Is Unlikely You Will Be Able to Satisfactorily Perform the Field Sobriety Tests

Unless a person has good balance and coordination, they are likely not going to pass field sobriety tests. These tests are designed to fail; the stances involved and movements required are unnatural and most people can't perform them to an officer's satisfaction, especially the older a person is. Current studies show most persons age 40 and over fail the tests, without having any alcohol in their system.

There is no law that requires a person suspected of DUI to perform field sobriety tests.*Yet people feel that they have to do everything that the officer tells them to do. But the reality is, if a person elects not to perform the field sobriety tests, the officer can't say the person failed them. It is important to remember that field sobriety tests are designed to fail.

There are no independent peer reviewed scientific studies that were conducted when the standardized field sobriety tests were developed to show that the tests determine whether a person is impaired. Field sobriety tests are another example of law enforcement pseudoscience.

**Note: A person that is on probation for a prior DUI conviction may have a probation term requiring the person to perform field sobriety tests if requested by an officer.*

A Person Does Not Have to Agree to Take a Preliminary Alcohol Screen Breath Test (PAS).*

Another misconception is that people feel they are compelled to blow into a preliminary alcohol screen (PAS) breath test device. In California a person does not have to agree to blow into a PAS breath test device *UNLESS the person is under 21 years of age OR the person is on probation for a prior DUI conviction.

In the investigation stage, the officer always wants the person to blow into the PAS breath device. Always remember that the PAS breath test is completely voluntary (except for the two exceptions noted above).

In fact, in California, the officer is mandated by law (Vehicle Code 23612(i)) to advise the driver that the test is voluntary and that the driver has the right to elect not to take the test. Unfortunately, many officers will not tell you that even though the admonition is required by law.

Which Test Can You Refuse without Consequence? When Are There Consequences for Refusing a Chemical Test?

Interviewer: I'm sure people are confused that they can refuse the roadside breath test, but the one administered at the police station has different consequences for refusing, is that correct?

Manuel Barba: During the DUI investigation the officer wants to ask the person questions about drinking alcohol etc. Every person has a right to remain silent and not say anything that would incriminate them.

During the DUI investigation the officer wants the person to perform Field Sobriety Tests. The person does not have to agree to do these agility tests, unless it is required by a term of probation resulting from a previous DUI conviction.

During the DUI investigation the officer will ask the person to blow into a Preliminary Alcohol Screen (PAS) Breath Test. As discussed above, the person does not have to blow into the PAS device, UNLESS the person is under 21 years of age OR if the person is currently on probation for a prior DUI conviction.

After the driver elects not to answer questions, elects not perform Field Sobriety Tests, and elects not to blow into the PAS breath test, the officer has to decide whether he is going to arrest the driver anyway (and he will).

In California, once the person is arrested, the person MUST submit to a chemical test, either a breath test or a blood test. Which test the person takes is usually their choice, assuming that both tests are available. **My advice to people is always take a blood test and never blow into any breath testing machine.**

Breath Test Machines and Alcohol Absorption

The biggest problem with breath testing machines (PAS included) is that they will always overstate the results if the person is still absorbing the alcohol that they drank.

Still absorbing means that there is still alcohol in the person's stomach and/or small intestine, and the alcohol continues to absorb into the blood stream; the alcohol level in the blood is still rising.

The science of breath testing assumes that the person is *fully absorbed* of all of the alcohol that the person drank, in order for the breath test machine results to accurately determine how much alcohol is in the person's blood stream. *Fully absorbed of the alcohol* means that there is no more alcohol in the person's stomach or small intestine; all of the alcohol has been absorbed into the person's blood stream and the alcohol level has reached equilibrium.

Equilibrium means that all of the alcohol is equally distributed throughout the person's body; so if a blood sample was drawn from the person's earlobe, and a second sample was drawn from the person's toe, and both samples were analyzed, the results for both samples would be essentially the same. This is because the alcohol throughout the body is equal (equilibrium).

Breath testing is deemed to be reliable when a person's alcohol content has reached equilibrium.

The problem is, if a person blows into a breath test machine before reaching the equilibrium stage, meaning that the person is still absorbing the alcohol, the breath test machine will overstate the results by two to three times. That's a big number! For instance, the machine result might show a 0.15%, but in reality the person's blood alcohol concentration is only a 0.05% or a 0.07%.

The reason for this problem is that it takes time for a person to absorb the alcohol that they drank.

When a person drinks alcohol, it first travels down the throat, then down the esophagus into the stomach. The alcohol then mixes in the stomach with any content in the stomach (i.e., food) and will eventually leave the stomach via the pyloric valve into the duodenum. The alcohol then enters the small intestine where it is absorbed into the blood stream entering the hepatic portal vein, where it is then transported to the liver.

Once the alcohol enters the hepatic portal vein, it of course mixes with the blood and is transported to the liver. The alcohol rich blood then enters the inferior vena cava, which is the large vein that carries *deoxygenated* blood from the lower half of the body into the right atrium of the heart located at the lower right, back side of the heart.

Once in the heart, the blood moves from the right atrium through the tricuspid valve into the right ventricle, and enters the pulmonary artery; the alcohol rich deoxygenated blood is now pumped to the lungs via the pulmonary artery.

Once this alcohol rich blood enters the lungs, it is oxygenated, and then returns to the heart via the pulmonary vein by entering the left atrium of the heart; the blood then goes through the mitral valve entering the left ventricle of the heart, and then is pumped into the aorta which then carries the alcohol rich now oxygenated blood simultaneously through the systemic veins to arteries, capillaries, organs and tissues in the body, including the liver.

From the aorta, the alcohol rich and now oxygenated blood also travels through the carotid arteries in the neck to the brain. Remember, a person becomes *impaired* by alcohol when the alcohol finally reaches the brain, and not before.

The brain controls a person's thought processes, including judgment, which is affected by the alcohol (mental impairment). The brain also controls the nervous system which controls muscles, and is also affected by the alcohol (physical impairment).

After reaching the brain the alcohol blood mixture returns the heart and continues to circulate throughout the entire body until the liver eventually removes all of the alcohol from the blood, which takes time.

The point of this mini human anatomy discussion is to point out the fact that it takes time for alcohol to absorb into the blood stream and reach the state of equilibrium throughout the body.

If a person drinks alcohol on an empty stomach, there is no food in the stomach so that alcohol enters the small intestine much faster and absorbs into the blood stream sooner.

If a person has food in his/her stomach and drinks alcohol, the food must digest before the alcohol can exit the stomach and enter the small intestine to absorb into the blood stream.

Scientific studies show that it can take up to six hours to be fully absorbed of the consumed alcohol. The amount of food in the stomach, the type of food, a person's ability to digest, the amount of alcohol consumed, as well as the type of alcohol consumed (beer, wine, liquor) are some of the factors that affect the time it takes for a person to absorb all of the alcohol they drank.

It is difficult, if not impossible, for a person to know whether or not he/she has fully absorbed all of the alcohol that was consumed. If not fully absorbed, then the person is still in the absorption stage.

If a person drinks a couple of glasses of wine and finished an hour ago, the person is likely still absorbing the alcohol into his/her blood stream. If the person drank the wine with dinner, the time it will take to absorb the alcohol into the blood stream has now increased.

Remember, studies show it can take up to six hours for a person to absorb alcohol, depending on whether the person has food in their stomach, what type of food, how much food, etc.

Thus, if a person is suspected of DUI, my advice is to always decline the breath test and always request a blood test. This is because (as stated above) breath test machines will always overstate the results if a person is still absorbing the consumed alcohol (the person has not reached equilibrium).

Why will the breath machine result always overstate the blood alcohol concentration? Recall the human anatomy discussion above? During the absorption of alcohol into the blood stream, the alcohol absorbs from the small intestine into the blood stream, it then travels to the heart, and is then pumped to the lungs so the blood can be oxygenated. Once the alcohol rich blood reaches the lungs, the lung tissues are now saturated with alcohol molecules which are transferred to the breath. So if a person blows into a breath test machine, the machine will get a breath sample that is rich in alcohol molecules - which results in a high reading! However, the alcohol has not reached equilibrium in the person's body. Remember the science of alcohol breath testing requires that the alcohol in person reach equilibrium, meaning the alcohol is distributed equally throughout a person's body. If a person has not reached equilibrium, the breath test machine is not being employed properly.

Again, because a person doesn't know whether they have fully absorbed the alcohol that they drank, they should never blow into a breath test machine, and instead request a blood test.

As a side note, blood alcohol analysis is by no means perfect either. Many things can go wrong with blood alcohol analysis as well.

Is It Common to Experience Certain Emotions after a DUI Arrest?

Interviewer: What have you learned about people's behavior, their reaction to being arrested for DUI? What human insights have you gained into this whole process?

There Is a Social Stigma about Being Arrested for Drinking and Driving

Manuel Barba: At first, most of the people I talk to are in shock. Most people believe that there's no way that they are guilty, meaning that they were not impaired or had an alcohol level of 0.08% or more. The fact that they were arrested puts them into shock. Then after they get over the shock, then I think the emotion evolves more toward a little bit of anger. They are angry at themselves for getting in this situation, for not knowing about their rights at the time they were stopped, and angry with the cop because the cop may have lied to them about doing this or that.

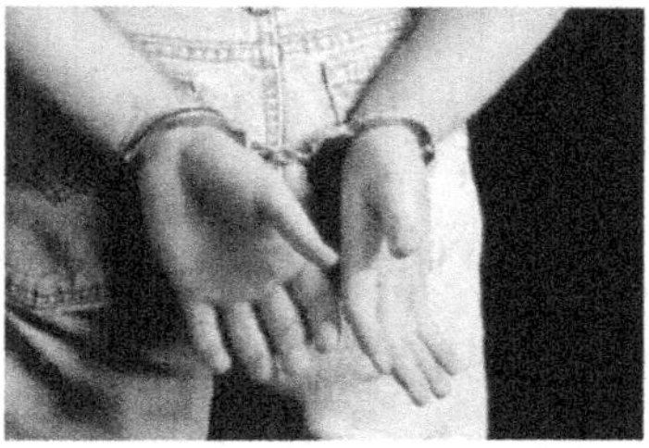

Then, there is also shame. They don't want other people to know that they were arrested for DUI. This is because the imagined implication that they must have a drinking problem. People don't realize that it doesn't take much to get arrested for a DUI.

Your Consultation with an Attorney Is Completely Confidential

Of course, I'm an attorney, so when people come to me and talk to me it's all confidential; no one is going to know that a person talked to me about a DUI arrest; no one is going to know who my clients are.

Disbelief is another stage that persons arrested for DUI go through. They just can't believe it happened... *"I only drank a couple of beers... I felt fine…I would never have driven if I didn't feel fine."* They are truly in disbelief.

Then, as the case progresses and all of the evidence has been gathered and analyzed, their emotions again shift to anger because they now see the flaws in the case against them.

Some people believe they should fight the DUI charge to the end because they feel that they are being wrongly accused. Other people decide to take the best deal I can get for them because the evidence doesn't looks so good. I think people experience different emotions along the way throughout the progression of the case.

The key is to hire a lawyer that is an expert in DUI defense; hire a lawyer that understands field sobriety tests; hire a lawyer that understands the science behind blood testing and breath testing. You need to hire a lawyer-scientist if you want to get the best possible resolution of your case.

Is the DUI Arrest going to become Public Knowledge?

Interviewer: How public is someone's situation going to be? Will work, friends, and family find out about their arrest?

Manuel Barba: Well, any arrest is public record. The fact that someone was arrested for DUI is public record and there are private companies that publish and sell that information.

Whether or not an employer is going to find out will depend on the type of job that the person has, as well as the arresting officer. Some officers will call the employer up and say, "Hey, by the way, I arrested your employee for DUI last night."

Interviewer: They really do that?

Manuel Barba: They don't all do it, but some do. I had a client that was a teacher and the arresting officer took it upon himself to call the school where the person taught and told the principal about the DUI arrest. Now, this was not some serious DUI arrest where there was an auto accident or an unusually high BAC. It was a very basic DUI arrest. It was just one of those situations where the client had a little wine with dinner and she ends up getting arrested for a DUI. The arresting officer called the principal of the school the next day and told him "*Teacher X was arrested for DUI last night*"

This was a well-respected teacher; the principal and the people from her school backed her up and supported her. A basic DUI charge is not something that will cause the teacher to lose her teaching credential anyway, so what was the point? Why did the officer do that, other than to try to humiliate this individual?

Interviewer: That's not slander or libel?

Manuel Barba: Not really, because if you think about it, it was the truth. She did get arrested for a DUI. But because someone is arrested does not necessarily mean that the person is guilty of a crime. People get arrested all the time and they're not guilty. In this country, an accused person remains innocent unless they are proven guilty beyond reasonable doubt by the government. That's a far cry from just getting arrested.

The California Department of Motor Vehicle Will Notify Commercial Drivers' Employers after a DUI Arrest

There are instances where notifications have to be made. The Department of Motor Vehicles has what are called "pull notices" with some employers because this person drives, for example, a tractor trailer truck.

If their license is confiscated because of a DUI arrest, that employer is going to get notified by the DMV right away. There are practical reasons for those types of notifications, but not everyone is subject to them.

Court records are generally public record. If someone knows about the DUI arrest they can search through the court records, assuming the court has online access, but most of the time other people are not going to know about the arrest unless they are told.

Can You Expect to Receive Mercy from the Court if You Plead Guilty?

Interviewer: Do you have people say to you, "Maybe I should just plead guilty and get it over with? "What would your advice be?

A DUI Charge can be Very Defensible

Manuel Barba: That's one of the myths of DUI. It is also one of the misconceptions. There are people out there that believe: they drank, and then drove, and then got arrested, so they must be guilty.

Well, the fact that a person drank alcohol, then drove a car, and then got arrested, does not mean anything. Remember, it's not illegal to drink alcohol and then drive a car.

To be guilty of a crime, the person must be either "*under the influence*" of the alcohol at the time of driving, and/or the person has to have an alcohol concentration of 0.08% or more at the time of driving. Both "*under the influence*" and "*driving while having a BAC of 0.08% or more*" are conclusions that must be proved by the government with evidence that is reliable, and it must be proved beyond a reasonable doubt.

An Experienced Attorney Can Analyze the Evidence to Uncover Weakness in the Prosecutor's Case

Those are the questions: Is this evidence reliable? Was the person's BAC 0.08% or more at the time of driving?

Was the person "under the influence" at the time of driving?

There are many factors that a qualified lawyer that is an expert in DUI defense must analyze in a case: the reasons for the stop, the driving observations, the stopping sequence, the initial contact by the officer, the exit of the vehicle, the DUI investigation including field sobriety test administration and performance, analysis of the chemical test results—by careful analysis of these factors, a qualified DUI defense attorney may find a way out.

There are people that think: *"If I just go in to court, plead guilty, and be done with it, I will be finished."* This is true. The person will be finished because the person will be convicted of a DUI and their driving privileges will have been suspended. The DUI conviction will be on their driving record for a minimum of 10 years. The person's auto insurance premiums will likely increase, or perhaps their insurance will be cancelled. And the person will now have a criminal record which can affect future employment opportunities.

But the real question is, was the person really guilty? Without analyzing all of the evidence, there is no way to know the answer to that question. Through the analysis of the evidence is where the defenses become apparent.

I have had many cases where, by reading what the officer wrote in the arrest report, and reading the chemical test results, the client looks guilty.

Well, arresting officers tend to embellish what they write in the arrest reports. They are rarely objective. Why? Because they are trying to support the fact that they arrested the person and they want to see the person convicted of DUI.

So unless a person has a qualified attorney analyze everything, and I mean everything, the person will never know where the problems are in their case.

Even if the person thinks they might be guilty of DUI, problems with the evidence in the case may surface during the investigation that will make it difficult for the prosecution to convict the person for DUI. Remember the ultimate question is can the government prove guilt beyond a reasonable doubt with evidence that is reliable.

Will the Department of Motor Vehicles (DMV) take action against a person's driver license if arrested for DUI?

Remember when arrested for a DUI, there are two separate proceedings that occur. First, the court is going to try to punish the arrested person for violating the law. Second, the Department of Motor Vehicles (DMV) is going to try to suspend the person's driving privilege through an administrative hearing process called the Administrative Per Se hearing.

The following is a brief summary of the DMV action that will take place:

Temporary License: When a person is arrested for DUI, the arresting officer will give the person a (Pink) document called the **Administrative Per Se Suspension/Revocation Order and Temporary License**. This is a 30 day temporary license that must be carried when driving after the arrest. It is a temporary license given to the arrested person because the arresting officer would have confiscated the person's California driver license when they were arrested. This temporary license is not a restricted license and the person can drive as normal.

If the person was driving with an out of state license, the arresting officer will not confiscate the out of state license but will give the person the pink temporary license / order of suspension. Keep in mind that even if the arrested person does not have a California driver license, the DMV can still suspend the person's privilege to drive in California with the person's out of state license.

The pink temporary license is also a notice to the arrested person that their driving privilege will be suspended in 30 days from the date of arrest and that the arrested person has 10 days to request a hearing with the DMV to contest the license suspension.

Requesting DMV Hearing: A person arrested for a DUI has 10 days from the date of receiving the pink temporary license/order of suspension to request a hearing with the DMV. The DMV hearing is ***essential*** as it is the only way to contest the driving privilege suspension.

Important Note: If the person arrested for DUI fails to request a DMV hearing within the initial 10 days from the date of arrest, the hearing rights may be deemed waived by the DMV and the suspension will go into effect automatically when the 30 day pink temporary license expires.

After the DMV hearing is requested, and the hearing is scheduled outside of 30 days from the arrest date (and it usually is), all action against the person's driving privilege will be "stayed" or stopped. In other words,

NO action will be taken against the person's driving privilege until the DMV hearing process is completed and the DMV rules on the case.

Once the DMV hearing is requested, the arrested person will receive another temporary license in the mail from the DMV before the Pink temporary license expires. The arrested person will be able to continue to drive normally until the DMV hearing process has been completed and the DMV issues their ruling—the Findings and Decision.

The Administrative Per Se (APS) Hearing: The APS hearing will be held at one of the regional DMV Driver Safety offices before a DMV hearing officer, who is a DMV employee.

Depending on what city the person was arrested in for DUI, the person's APS hearing will be assigned to one of the statewide DMV Driver Safety offices.

In a typical alcohol DUI case, the DMV hearing officer has to decide three issues:

- Was the person driving?
- Were they lawfully arrested?
- Was the person's Blood Alcohol Concentration .08% or higher at the time of driving?

To suspend the person's driving privilege, the DMV must prove all three of the above issues with evidence that is admissible and reliable by a "preponderance" of the evidence, which means "more likely than not."

In order to win this hearing, the driver (through his qualified DUI Defense attorney) must show that one or more of the above issues is not true. We do this by: gathering all of the evidence, analyzing it to determine the strengths and weaknesses, contesting the DMV's evidence, and presenting affirmative evidence where applicable.

DMV APS hearings are somewhat informal; however, they follow legal evidentiary rules.

There are factual, legal, and technical issues that must be examined. We must review the officer's arrest report, the arresting officer's sworn statement (DS367), and chemical test results, as well as the documentation supporting the chemical test results – these documents make up the DMV's case against the driver arrested for DUI.

My office will likely subpoena various records related to the arresting officer's initial contact, the DUI investigation, chemical test results, and other evidence, which may include documents, audio/video recordings, as well as live witnesses.

Because the issues in DUI cases differ from one another, the evidence needed to defend each case at the DMV hearing also differ. The driver may also be needed to testify at the DMV hearing.

In my opinion, although it is the driver's right to attend the APS hearing, I usually recommend that the driver not be present at the DMV hearing, unless we need his or her testimony. The reason for this is that if the driver is present, the DMV hearing officer can call the driver as a witness and question the driver. Therefore being present is something I do not advise in many cases.

After the conclusion of the DMV APS hearing, the DMV will issue their ruling called the "Findings and Decision." A "set aside" means that the driver has won, and there will be no license suspension. If the hearing is lost, the Findings and Decision will advise when the suspension of the driving privilege will go into effect and for how long. Typically the suspension will begin several days after you receive the notice of Findings and Decision.

For a first time DUI arrest, the DMV will suspend the driving privilege for a four month period, but a person has the option to get a restricted license to drive after the first 30 days of the four month suspension if certain requirements are met (enroll in alcohol class, file proof of insurance with DMV, pay reissuance fee).

But on a second and third DUI within 10 years, the DMV will suspend the driving privilege for a minimum of 1 year. And that's a long time, so it is in the driver's best interest to fight the case with a qualified DUI defense attorney.

I have had many clients hire me for their second DUI arrest, and when I ask them: "*What happened on your first DUI?* The client says, "*Well, I didn't think it was a big deal so I just went in and pled guilty.*"

Well it's a big deal now because the person now has a prior DUI and the DMV is going to try to suspend the driving privilege for a minimum of 1 year, and the person can't get a restricted license until after the 1 year suspension.

Hiring an Experienced DUI Defense Attorney to Defend a DUI May Result in the Charge Being Reduced and Avoiding the License Suspension for a Subsequent Offense

A first time DUI is a big deal, but a second DUI is even more problematic because the penalties from the court and the DMV increase greatly.

I always counsel people to fight their first DUI arrest, because if successful, it won't be there to become a "prior" DUI.

There are a number of things that can happen by fighting a DUI. The charge might be dismissed on a Fourth Amendment issue, the charge might be reduced to a non-DUI related charge through a plea deal, or the person could win at trial and be found not guilty. If the case is not properly analyzed, a person will never know if problems with the evidence exist; and if a person doesn't know what the problems are associated with their DUI case, how can they get the best resolution for their case?

Interviewer: So a first offense DUI should be taken very seriously.

Manuel Barba: In my opinion, ANY arrest for DUI should be taken seriously. There are a number of defenses that may surface. DUI cases are not "open and shut" cases. DUI cases are very complex, but they can be very defensible. That's why it is essential to hire an attorney that is an expert in DUI defense.

If a person hires a lawyer that pretends to defend DUI cases, the lawyer is likely going to plead the client guilty. If that is the person's goal, they should just go to court and plead themselves guilty, because the outcome will be the same. I refer to lawyers that pretend to defend DUI cases *escort service attorneys*, because the attorney escorts the client to the judge with the plea documents.

DUIs in Southern California are Subject to Mandatory Sentencing Guidelines

Interviewer: As a related question, is there truly any mercy of the courts that people can throw themselves on? Or are the courts unsympathetic? Does it matter if you're a good person, you have a family, and this is your first time?

First Offense DUI Convictions May Be Subject to Jail and a 4 or 9 Month Alcohol Education Class

Manuel Barba: For DUIs in Southern California, the sentencing is pretty straightforward. In other words, it's mandatory. Depending on what court and what county a person is in; there may be some differences in that some courts add to the penalties. It's not something that a person is going to get away with. If a person comes into court and pleads guilty, and they have no prior DUI convictions, the person is going to get sentenced accordingly, for a first time DUI treatment for that court.

Depending on the blood alcohol concentration, a person will be ordered to complete either a four month or nine month alcohol class. Depending on the court there may be some jail time involved, which can be served straight time, weekend work release, electronic monitoring, or community service, depending on what court and county the person is in. The minimum jail sentence on a first time DUI is 0 days in jail, and the maximum is 6 months in jail. What a person actually is sentenced to will depend on the facts of the case. Even if a person gets no jail, the person is still convicted of a DUI.

In addition, most Courts order the person to be on summary probation for three years, and there are fines that can amount to about $2000 or more, depending on the court and county. Some courts add on other additional classes or AA meetings depending on the case. The fact that a person does not have any prior DUI convictions is the reason why they are only getting sentenced based on first time DUI terms, so trying to argue that the person has never been in trouble before doesn't usually help that much.

Los Angeles County Requires Drivers to Install an Ignition Interlock Device for a First Offense

The California Legislature (AB91) required the Department of Motor Vehicles to implement a pilot program in four counties requiring the installation of Ignition Interlock Devices (IID) on all cars owned by persons convicted of a first DUI as well as multiple DUI offenders. The program went into effect July 01, 2010 and is scheduled to end December 31, 2015 unless extended (which will likely happen). The purpose of the program is to study the effectiveness of IIDs in reducing repeat DUI offenses.

Thus, if a person is convicted of a DUI - even for a first time DUI - in one of these counties: Alameda, Los Angeles, Sacramento, or Tulare, the Department of Motor Vehicles (DMV) will require that an IID be installed on all cars that the person owns or operates. It does not matter what county a person lives in, as the requirement focuses on what county a person was *convicted* in.

For example, a person convicted of a first time DUI in Los Angeles County, but lives in Riverside County, must install the IID. However, a person who lives in Los Angeles County, but was convicted of a DUI in Riverside County, no IID is required UNLESS the court required it for some different reason.

Ignition Interlock Devices require the driver to blow into the device to ensure the driver is alcohol free before the car engine will start. Once started, the IID device will require that the driver blow into the device periodically while driving. If the IID device detects alcohol, the car will not start.

The politics behind the IID program go something like this: the manufacturers of the fuel cell technology used in these IID devices give money to organizations like Mothers Against Drunk Driving (MADD), who in turn give campaign money to the lawmakers, who in turn pass these types of laws.

Again, I am not saying drinking an excessive amount of alcohol and driving a car is a good thing - clearly it is not. But there are better ways to deal with problem DUI offenders. Studies show most persons convicted of a first time DUI do not get another DUI in the future as they have learned their lesson.

The problem with installing an IID on every car owned by a person convicted of a first time DUI is a bit draconian, especially when studies show that most first time offenders do not re-offend. The real motivation here is making money for the manufacturers of the IID devices.

My prediction is that in 2014-2015 there will be a push in the California Legislature to expand the IID program statewide.

Unfortunately DUI legislation is driven by money and politics; "public safety" is just the rouse used by politicians to get public support.

Is Self-Representation or a Public Defender a Viable Option to Defend a DUI Charge?

Interviewer: Do people say, "Well, do I even need a lawyer? What if I just try to represent myself or just go get a public defender or a general criminal defense lawyer?

Why Is DUI Defense So Specialized?

Manuel Barba: As to representing one's own case, the question is does the person accused of DUI have the expertise to defend his/her own DUI case?

Does the person understand the protocols related to a DUI investigation?

Does the person understand the development of Field Sobriety Tests?

Does the person understand human kinetics (the science of human movement) and how it relates to Field Sobriety Tests?

Does the person understand the pharmacokinetics of alcohol or the specific drug that they are accused of being under the influence of? (Pharmacokinetics deals with how the drug interacts with the body once ingested).

Does the person understand the pharmacodynamics of alcohol or the specific drug that they are accused of being under the influence of? (Pharmacodynamics deals with how the drug affects the human body).

Does the person understand the science behind breath testing analysis and/or blood testing analysis as it relates to their specific case?

Does the person understand the law as it relates to their particular case?

And more importantly, does the person have the objectivity to apply all of the above knowledge to their own case?

Manuel Barba: As to the second question of having a public defender or a general criminal defense lawyer handle the defense of a DUI case, the question is: does the lawyer have the expertise to defend a DUI case?

Now, I don't mean does the lawyer have the knowledge to appear in court, get an offer from the judge or district attorney, fill out plea forms, and escort the accused person to the judge and plead them guilty to a DUI charge; any lawyer can do that. In fact the accused person can do those things themselves (with the exception of filling out the proper forms)!

When I ask the question: does the lawyer have the expertise to *defend* a DUI case? I am really asking:

Does the lawyer understand the protocols related to a DUI investigation?

Does the lawyer understand the development of Field Sobriety Tests and understand human kinetics and how it relates to Field Sobriety Tests?

Does the lawyer understand the pharmacokinetics of alcohol or the specific drug that the person is accused of being under the influence of?

Does the lawyer understand the pharmacodynamics of alcohol or the specific drug that that the person is accused of being under the influence of?

Does the lawyer understand the science behind breath testing analysis and/or blood testing analysis as it relates specifically to the client's DUI case?

Does the lawyer understand the law as it relates specifically to that particular case?

And more importantly, does the lawyer have the ability to competently defend the person's DUI case *through trial* if necessary?

Criminal Defense Lawyer does not necessarily mean DUI Defense Lawyer

It is true that DUI defense is a subcategory of criminal defense in general. But even if a lawyer works in criminal defense, that doesn't necessarily mean that the lawyer has the expertise to defend a DUI case. To properly defend a DUI case, the lawyer must have specialized knowledge with regard to all of the areas I mentioned on the previous pages.

The lawyer must not only know the science, but know it and understand it better than the prosecutor, the cop, and the state criminalist, and be prepared to take the case to trial if necessary.

Understand that appearing in court, getting an offer from the judge or prosecutor, filling out plea forms, and escorting the accused person to the judge and pleading them guilty to a DUI charge is NOT *defending* a DUI case. That is nothing more than pleading the client guilty, which is something the client can do themselves.

If the lawyer does not understand all of the science related to defending a DUI, the lawyer is not going to be able to attack the evidence that the government will use to claim the accused person is guilty.

If all the lawyer is going to do is look at the chemical test results and say to the accused person: *"the results say your BAC was 0.15%, (or whatever) you better plead guilty."* That is not defending and is truly a disservice to the accused person. What if the chemical test is wrong, etc.?

Public Defenders Generally Lack the Specialized Knowledge of a DUI Defense Attorney

Many Public Defenders are very good lawyers, but they are usually overworked, and their office lacks the resources to properly train them in the intricacies and science related to DUI defense. Public Defenders handle many different types of cases so they usually lack the expertise necessary to defend a DUI case.

Now this is not to say that a Public Defender can't help a person accused of DUI. Some DUI cases are less complicated than others, and there are some Public Defenders that get great results negotiating a disposition and at trial.

But there are also many Public Defenders that just want to move the case through the court system with the least amount of effort. The bottom line is the person accused of DUI is probably going to get convicted of a DUI because the Public Defender is going to plead them guilty.

When a person accused of DUI hires an attorney that is an expert in DUI defense, they are hiring someone that has (or should have) the specialized knowledge in all the areas I mentioned a few pages back, and as a result the person accused of DUI will have a better chance at getting the best possible result.

A Public Defender Will Not Represent You at the DMV Administrative Hearing

Interviewer: In terms of the DUI, though, there's a criminal side, but there's also a non-criminal administrative hearing for the driver's license. Can a Public Defender even address that part of if the case?

Manuel Barba: No, and they do not. When a person is arrested for DUI, there are two separate proceedings. One is the administrative side of it, where the Department of Motor Vehicles (DMV) is going to suspend the driver license. That's the DMV's goal.

Public Defenders don't handle the DMV side of the DUI case, so the driver license will be suspended if not defended properly.

Then you have the criminal side, where the Court wants to punish the person arrested for DUI for allegedly breaking the law. A lawyer that is an expert in DUI defense can handle both the DMV aspect of the case as well as the Court case, and more importantly coordinate both defenses to get the best possible outcome.

A DUI Defense Attorney Can Discover Valuable Information at the DMV Hearing and then Incorporate it into the Court Case Defense

Personally, I like to use the DMV license hearing as a discovery tool, to gather evidence to use in defending the DMV case, which then gives me valuable insights in defending the court case. In essence I know what the evidence is going to show because I've dealt with it at the DMV hearing. This can be very valuable.

Since Public Defenders don't handle DMV license hearings, they are not going to have that benefit of uncovering information from the DMV hearing that can help the client in the court case.

WHAT QUALITIES SHOULD YOU LOOK FOR WHEN CONSIDERING RETAINING AN ATTORNEY TO DEFEND A DUI CHARGE?

Interviewer: What would you do if you were arrested for DUI? How would you find the right attorney? What would you look for?

Manuel Barba: Knowing what I know, of course, I'm going to hire an attorney that is an expert in DUI defense; one that knows the science related to DUI cases inside and out. I would want a lawyer that understands DUI investigations from the police officer's perspective; a lawyer that knows field sobriety tests inside and out.

I would want a lawyer-scientist that understands how alcohol affects the human body, and understand the science of breath testing and blood testing. I would want an attorney that is thorough, leaving no stone unturned in the investigation and analysis of the evidence in the case. I would want an attorney that is aggressive when needed, as well as a good negotiator.

I would NOT want an attorney that is going to take my money, hold my hand, and plead me guilty to the court.

Experience in Analyzing the Evidence Is Vital to DUI Defense

The evidence is everything. What does it mean? An attorney that is an expert in DUI defense is going to analyze everything in the case. Everything includes the events that led to the police officer making contact with the citizen. If it was a traffic stop, what was the driving like? Why did the officer stop the driver? Is there an issue with the validity of the stop itself? Was the stop due to some sort of bad driving? Or was the stop due to a non-driving issue, such as expired registration, tinted windows, etc.

Once the officer's red lights came on, how did the driver react? What was the stopping sequence like? What were the officer's observations during the initial contact with the driver? When the officer told the driver to get out of the car, what was the exit sequence like? Did the driver answer questions or make incriminating statements?

Did the officer administer field sobriety tests? If so, which tests? What were the instructions given to the driver? How did the driver perform?

Did the officer administer a preliminary alcohol screen (PAS) breath test? Did the officer follow all of the procedures in administering the PAS breath test? Was an evidential breath test or blood test performed? Were all the procedures followed? Is the blood test analysis reliable?

The foregoing questions illustrate a general outline for a typical DUI investigation, but there are many sub-issues that exist for each of the questions I asked. This is why it is essential to hire an attorney that is an expert in DUI defense if arrested for DUI.

Here is an analogy: A DUI case is like having cancer. If a person has cancer, and they go to a cut-rate doctor that takes the person's temperature and gives them an aspirin, the person is probably not going to survive from the cancer.

The person with cancer needs to go to the best cancer specialist possible, to have the best chance of surviving the cancer. The cancer specialist is going to give the cancer patient the best chance of surviving because of his/her specialized knowledge.

The same is true with a DUI case. There are DUI cases where there are many defenses because of issues that we are able to find by thoroughly investigating the case and analyzing the evidence.

Then there are cases that have few, if any, defenses because of the strength of the evidence against the client.

But until a thorough investigation of all of the facts is completed and all of the evidence is analyzed, there is no way of knowing where the problems are.

Can You Afford to Hire an Experienced DUI Defense Attorney or Can you Afford NOT to?

Interviewer: I've seen news and advertisements that say, a DUI conviction can cost a person about $15,000-$20,000 if they don't fight the case and plead guilty. But if they fight the case by hiring an expert DUI defense attorney, it could cost less? Would you say that is accurate?

Manuel Barba: The government puts out a lot of propaganda in the form of public service announcements. I think that it could realistically cost that much, but not necessarily. But then it could cost much more. It really depends on the person, what their job is, etc.

I have represented clients that were on the verge of losing their job, etc. If they lose their job, they can lose their house and everything else. What is the value of all this potential loss?

There is an old saying: good lawyers aren't cheap, and cheap lawyers aren't good.

Hiring a good attorney is an investment. I've represented a number of persons where their livelihood was on the line. I have represented commercial truck drivers, firemen, paramedics, police detectives, doctors, dentists, lawyers and teachers, and many other categories of persons, each with a different type of employment and different situations. My question to each client is usually the same: What is your goal and why? What do you want to accomplish with this representation?

Some clients want to get the best deal that they can get. Some clients have to win at all costs because of their job or some other issue regarding their personal life. They just cannot have a DUI conviction.

If a person does not fight their DUI arrest and they are convicted of DUI, they will have to pay court fines; they will have to pay the cost for the alcohol classes; the cost of the ignition interlock if applicable; the cost of higher insurance premiums for the next several years; they may even have to pay the cost of alternative transportation when they lose their driver license. And they will have the cost of lost employment opportunities because of the criminal record.

By hiring an attorney that is an expert in DUI defense, although it may not be cheap, a person accused of DUI may likely end up with a much better case resolution overall, including possibly a dismissal, reduced charges, or a not guilty verdict.

California DUIs Are Comprised of Two Charges: Having a BAC over the Legal Limit and Driving While "Under the Influence."

Interviewer: When someone's arrested, they're facing two charges? Driving Under the Influence and also Driving with a Blood Alcohol Concentration (BAC) of 0.08% or above?

Manuel Barba: That's correct. In California, a typical alcohol DUI arrest consists of two charges: Vehicle Code 23152(a) is "driving while under the influence of alcohol" and Vehicle Code 23152(b) "driving while having a blood alcohol concentration of 0.08% or more."

If the BAC level is below 0.08%, the prosecutor can charge the single charge of *"driving while under the influence of alcohol"* (Vehicle Code 23152(a)). Many people believe that if their BAC level is less than 0.08%, they are not in trouble. This is not correct. A person may have blown into a preliminary alcohol screen (PAS) breath test and had a result of 0.06%, and still be arrested for *driving while under the influence of alcohol* if there is evidence that the person is *impaired* by the alcohol, regardless of what the actual breath or blood test result is.

It doesn't matter what the number is. Remember, law enforcement officers are looking for DUI arrests.

The second charge, Vehicle Code 23152(b), is known as the *Per Se* charge, which is *"driving with a blood alcohol concentration of 0.08% or more."* The *per se* count is charged when the officer believes the chemical test result will be 0.08% or more.

With this charge, it doesn't matter whether the person is *impaired* by the alcohol. The only thing that matters is whether the person's blood alcohol concentration was 0.08% or more at the time of driving. The person can be completely sober, but if the person's BAC is 0.08% or more at the time of driving, the person can be charged with Vehicle Code 23152(b).

This is the government's way of trying to get a conviction two ways: either the person was *under the influence of alcohol at the time of driving*, or the person *drove with a BAC of 0.08% or more.*

Of course, the real issues are as follows: was the person truly *under the influence* of the alcohol at the time of driving? And was the person's blood alcohol concentration truly 0.08% or more *at the time of driving*? The defense of the case begins with these two questions, because they are factual conclusions that must be proven by the government with reliable evidence beyond reasonable doubt; which is not always so easy for the government to do when the defense is handled by an attorney who is an expert in DUI defense.

Is Your Driver License Immediately Confiscated after a DUI Arrest?

Interviewer: When someone's arrested for DUI in California, what about their driver's license? Is it taken immediately? Can you get a hardship or an occupational or a work license?

California Drivers with a BAC of 0.08% or Higher Have Their Licenses Confiscated; Out of State Drivers May Lose Their California Driving Privilege

Manuel Barba: Here's how it works: if a person is arrested for an alcohol related DUI, and there's evidence that the person's blood alcohol concentration (BAC) is 0.08% or more, the arresting officer will "snatch" the person's driver license at the time of the arrest.

If the driver is from out of state and does not have a California driver license, the officer cannot take the out of state driver license, as he has no authority to do so. But keep in mind the California Department of Motor Vehicles can still suspend the out of state driver's *privilege* to drive in California.

The Officer Provides You with a Temporary 30-Day License

After the arresting officer takes the California driver's license, the officer will give the driver a "pink" document from the Department of Motor Vehicles entitled "Administrative Per Se Suspension/Revocation Order and Temporary Driver License." This temporary license is good for 30 days, and after the 30 days a suspension will go into effect automatically. The length of the suspension depends upon whether or not the driver has prior DUI convictions and/or suspensions.

It is Essential to Request the DMV Hearing within 10 Days of Your Arrest

The "pink" temporary license also advises the driver that they have 10 days to request a hearing (Administrative Per Se hearing) to show that the suspension is not justified.

If the DMV hearing is not requested within 10 days, then the hearing rights are waived and the suspension will go into effect automatically.

It is always better to have the DUI defense attorney that will be defending the DUI case request the DMV hearing so that the driver makes no statements to the DMV. This also puts the DMV on notice as to who the attorney is.

When my firm requests a DMV hearing for a client, the DMV knows that we will be subpoenaing many records related to the case, which is going to take some time to get. In addition, my firm conducts all DMV hearings in person at the Driver Safety Office.

When a driver calls the DMV themselves to request a hearing, the DMV will usually set a telephonic hearing right away, which can limit the time to gather evidence.

Telephonic hearings are a mistake and the license will very likely be suspended as a result. Many lawyers that pretend to defend DUI cases conduct DMV hearings telephonically and don't subpoena any records or witnesses. How on earth can a lawyer examine the DMV's original documents over the phone? How can a lawyer rebut any of the DMV issues without subpoenaing and analyzing all of the evidence?

Once the DMV hearing is requested, all DMV action against the driver's driving privilege will stop (stayed) and the driver will be able to continue to drive as usual until the DMV hearing process is completed and a decision is reached as to whether the license will be suspended or the action against the driving privilege is set aside.

The issues at a typical DMV Administrative Per Se hearing are: (1) did the officer have reasonable cause to believe that the driver was driving while under the influence? (2) Was the driver lawfully arrested? And (3) was the driver's blood alcohol concentration 0.08% or more at the time of driving? It is the DMV's burden to prove that all three of these issues are true with evidence that is reliable and admissible at the DMV hearing by a preponderance of the evidence, which means more likely than not.

The DMV hearing is essential as it is the driver's only opportunity to contest the DMV suspension by contesting one or more of the above issues at the DMV hearing.

The DMV hearing gives the DUI Defense lawyer access to all of the evidence related to the DUI arrest. This includes all evidence related to the stop, the DUI investigation, chemical test results, as well as evidence related to the analysis of any blood samples. The DUI defense attorney can subpoena evidence and any witnesses as needed to rebut one or more of the above three issues.

Once the DMV hearing is requested, the defense of the DUI case begins. Even though the DMV hearing is separate from the court case, it still arises out of the same event (the DUI arrest) so the evidence gathered at the DMV hearing will give the lawyer insight into defending the court case. The two proceedings must be coordinated. It is essential to hire an attorney that is an expert in DUI defense to have the best possible chance of winning the DMV hearing so that the driving privilege is not suspended.

REFUSING THE BREATH OR BLOOD TEST

Interviewer: What happens if you refuse a breath test or blood test? Can you defend against a false classification of refusing?

California Is an Implied Consent State

Manuel Barba: Absolutely. In California, with regard to a refusal of the *evidential* chemical test (breath or blood test), there are certain procedures that an arresting officer must comply with before a driver can be charged with refusing the evidential chemical test.

California is an implied consent state, which means that, by having a driver's license, a driver has given his/her consent to submit to an evidential breath test or blood test if an officer arrests the driver for suspicion of DUI.

The driver is entitled to a DMV hearing to contest any refusal allegation. If the DMV finds that the driver did refuse, the driver license will be suspended for one year or more depending on the circumstances.

Now keep in mind that a refusal allegation only applies to the evidential chemical test after being arrested. A refusal allegation does not apply to the preliminary alcohol screen (PAS) breath test offered by an officer before the person is arrested, because the person has a right to elect not to blow into the PAS breath test.

During a DUI investigation, an officer often tries to get the person to blow into the PAS breath test to determine an alcohol level. This is a voluntary test and a person has a statutory right (VC23612 (i)) to refuse the PAS breath test. Note: *If the person is under the age of 21, submitting to the PAS breath test is mandatory. Also if the person is currently on probation for a prior DUI conviction, submitting to the PAS breath test is mandatory.*

But once a person is arrested for suspicion of DUI, the person must submit to a chemical test, either a breath test or a blood test, if they are both available. If the person refuses the *post-arrest* chemical test, then the refusal allegation applies and the DMV will attempt to suspend the driving privilege for at least one year.

If the officer fails to follow the proper procedures as far as advising the person that he/she can lose their driver license for a year or more if the person refuses the evidential chemical test, then the refusal allegation may be set aside by the DMV and the license will not be suspended.

Consciousness of Guilt

In addition, if a person refuses the evidential chemical test, the prosecutor could use evidence of the refusal in court to try to show the accused person's *consciousness of guilt.* The argument is that the person refused to take a chemical test because the person was trying to hide their guilt. This argument is not always successful, because a person may have refused for a number of reasons, including confusion caused by the arresting officer.

Factors That Can Enhance a DUI Charge

Interviewer: Are there other factors that will enhance a DUI charge?

Manuel Barba: That's correct. The prosecutor can allege enhancements when filing DUI charges that can lead to enhanced punishments.

• Refusing an evidential chemical test after being arrested for DUI can result in additional punishment.

• Driving with a child passenger under the age of 14 can result in additional DUI penalties.

• Driving over the speed limit by 30 miles per hour in a reckless manner can lead to enhanced DUI penalties.

• Having a blood alcohol concentration above 0.15% and 0.20% can also result in increased DUI punishment.

• Speeding through a construction zone can result in increased DUI penalties.

Sometimes prosecutors file enhancements to make the case look worse (over-charging) in an attempt to pressure the accused person to plead the case guilty: *"I will drop the enhancements if you plead guilty today."* Prosecutors have a duty to *do justice,* but some prosecutors have a strange definition of what justice is.

Under 0.08%: Will You Be Arrested If Your BAC Is Below the Legal Limit?

Interviewer: Are there any laws in California if someone has a BAC below 0.08%? Will they still arrest you?

You May Be Arrested Because You Still Meet the First Criteria of a DUI, Driving While Impaired

Manuel Barba: If a person is suspected of DUI, and their blood alcohol concentration is less than 0.08% an officer can still arrest the person for DUI. Remember the charge of VC23152 (a) is *driving while under the influence of alcohol.* All the officer needs is evidence that the person was *impaired.*

For instance, let's say a person blows into a preliminary alcohol screen (PAS) breath device and the result is .06%. The officer has the choice whether the person will be arrested for DUI. If the officer concludes that the person failed the field sobriety tests, meaning the person did not perform the tests as instructed, the officer will likely arrest the person for DUI, despite the fact that the PAS result was less than 0.08%. If the person did well on the field sobriety tests, the officer might let the person go (unlikely in my opinion as the officer wants to make a DUI arrest).

How a person performs on Field Sobriety Tests is very subjective. My advice is not to agree to perform the tests as they are completely voluntary. If a person elects not to perform the field sobriety tests, the officer can never say the person failed the tests.

The BAC result doesn't always mean much when the result is less than 0.08% because the ultimate question is "was the person impaired by the alcohol?"

Are Underage 21 Drivers Subject to Different DUI Laws?

Interviewer: What about drivers who are under age 21? What kind of BAC limits do they have?

Drivers under the Age of 21 Are Subject to a Zero Tolerance Policy; A BAC under 0.08% Will Result in a Year Long License Suspension

Manuel Barba: In California, there is a "zero tolerance" for alcohol policy for drivers under the age of 21.

First of all, by law an under age 21 driver MUST blow into a preliminary alcohol screen (PAS) breath test device if asked to do so by an officer who suspects that the underage driver has been drinking.

If the underage driver blows into the PAS device and the result is 0.01% or more, the underage driver can be charged with VC23136, which is an under 21 driver driving with a BAC of 0.01% or more. This crime is an infraction, punishable by fine only, however, the Department of Motor Vehicles (DMV) will try to suspend the driver license for a minimum of one year. The underage driver is entitled to a DMV administrative hearing and has 10 days to request a hearing.

In addition to the 0.01% or more charge (VC23136), if the underage driver blows into the PAS device and the result is 0.05% or more, the underage driver can be charged with VC23140, which is an under 21 driver driving with a BAC of 0.05% or more. This crime is also an infraction, punishable by fine only, however the Department of Motor Vehicles (DMV) will try to suspend the driver license for a minimum of one year. The underage driver is entitled to a DMV administrative hearing and has 10 days to request a hearing.

BAC Results of 0.08% or above Will Result in the Same DUI Charge an Adult Would Face

If an under age 21 driver has a PAS breath test result of 0.08% or more, the prosecutor will charge the driver with a typical DUI, just as if the person was 21 years of age or older.

If an under age 21 driver has a PAS breath test result of 0.08% or more, and was involved in an auto accident and someone was injured or killed, the underage driver will be charged with a felony, just as if the person was age 21 or over.

DRUG-RELATED DUI CHARGES

Interviewer: What percentage of the cases you see are due to illegal or prescription drugs versus alcohol? Are the drug cases harder to defend or more complicated?

Drug-Related DUIs: There Are No Per Se Laws Regulating the Impairment by Drugs

Manuel Barba: Drug cases are not necessarily harder to defend. In a way I think they're a little easier, because there is no per se law.

Originally DUIs were mostly alcohol related. The original DUI charge was for *driving under the influence*. There were people that were not under the influence, meaning they were not impaired by the alcohol, even while having a blood alcohol concentration (BAC) of 0.10%. The alcohol wasn't affecting them. Those people would be found not guilty, because that was the law at the time; the prosecution had to prove the person was driving while *under the influence*.

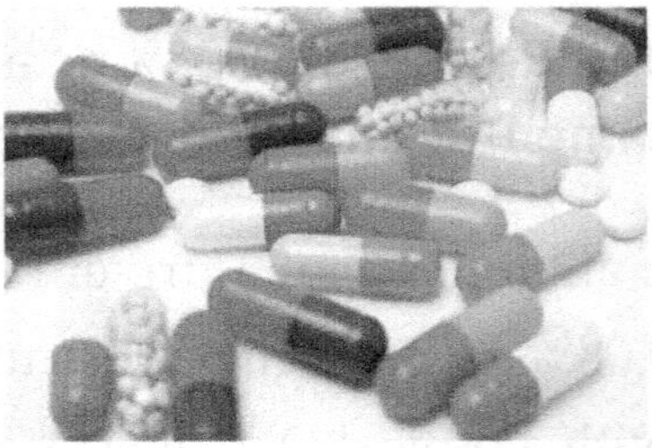

Thereafter, the government created the *per se* laws, which set a legal limit for blood alcohol concentration while driving. If a person drives with a blood alcohol concentration set by the *per se* laws, the person would be in violation of the law, and thus guilty of DUI. The original per se laws set the legal BAC limit at 0.15%. Thereafter the per se laws were changed to 0.10%.

Currently, due to pressure from the federal government, the per se laws were reduced to a BAC of 0.08%. Essentially, the federal government told the states that if they wanted to continue receiving highway funds from the federal government, the state must adopt the 0.08% BAC legal limit.

Thus it doesn't matter whether a person is impaired by the alcohol; if the person was driving and has a BAC of 0.08%, the person is guilty, even if the person is sober as day at the 0.08% level. Nevertheless, the question now is: was the person truly a 0.08% at the time of driving?

These per se laws are more about politics than they are about science, as there are no peer reviewed scientific studies that conclude that all persons are impaired at a blood alcohol concentration of 0.08%.

The point is, currently there are NO per se laws that apply to driving after taking a drug(s), whether they are illegal or prescription. When only drugs are involved, the question is: at the time of driving, was the driver *impaired* by the drug that they ingested?

The term "drugs" has a negative sound to it. However keep in mind that "drugs" does not necessarily mean illegal drugs. "Drugs" includes prescription medication that has been prescribed by a doctor.

California Has Been Trying to Enact Legislation Governing Drug Levels and Impairment

As mentioned earlier, currently there are no per se drug laws; but there are forces that are currently trying to have the legislature in Sacramento pass *per se* drug laws.

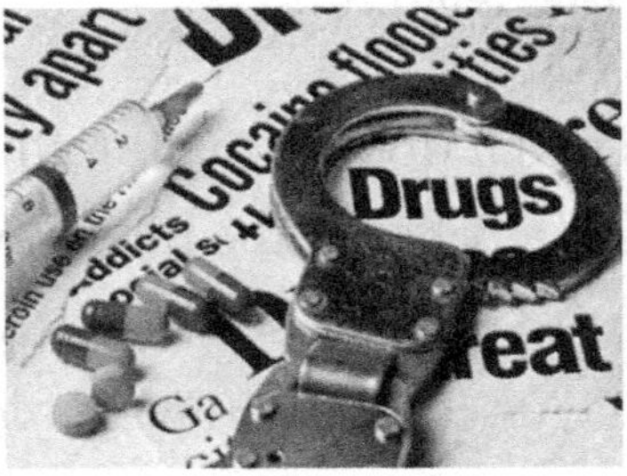

There was an attempt last year by the law enforcement community to get the California legislature to pass a per se drug law which in essence stated that if a driver had any drug in their body, any amount, that would be a per se violation of the law and the driver would be guilty.

What a ridiculous law! Can you imagine? Think of all the older people out there that are on their blood pressure and/or other medications.

What if a person drinks two cups of coffee and was then stopped by a cop? The person would have "an amount" of caffeine (which is a drug) in their body and would be guilty of DUI. Yes, that is crazy.

Not only am I a specialist member of the California DUI Lawyer's Association, but I am also a member of the Board of Directors. Our organization worked with our lobbyist and members of the scientific community to oppose this crazy law and provide testimony in Sacramento when the law was being considered. Luckily we were able to defeat the law so it never came to fruition.

Rest assured that the forces that want drug per se laws will not give up. Law enforcement lobbies are powerful in Sacramento and law enforcement agencies have learned how lucrative DUI arrests are. Remember, for every DUI arrest made, the law enforcement agency gets grant money. DUI has become a funding mechanism at the expense of the public. These ridiculous laws are packaged nicely and are sold to the unsuspecting public as a necessity to ensure *public safety*. And the public buys into it.

In addition, manufacturers in the private sector have developed devices that will "read" swabs from a driver's mouth, and the device will "confirm" the presence of substances that *may* be from a drug. These manufacturers are providing funding to get drug per se laws passed around the country so that the manufacturers can sell their new devices to law enforcement agencies. These "swab" reading devices are currently being used by law enforcements agencies today to try them out.

It's all about making money.

So it goes like this: When an officer stops a driver, and the driver says that he/she has not been drinking, the officer's next question is: *"have you been taking any medications?"* And the unsuspecting driver says: *"Yes, I've taken my prescription meds for [whatever the condition is]"* And the cop responds: *"Would you do some field sobriety test for me?"* And the unsuspecting driver says: *"Sure, I'm fine…"* The officer concludes that the driver doesn't perform the test as instructed. The officer then asks for a swab from the driver's inner cheek and it gets analyzed in the swab reading device and the result is positive. The driver is arrested, a blood sample is drawn, analyzed, and the results show the presence of metabolites that were created by the driver's body as it processed the prescribed medication.

The driver is then charged with DUI.

Per se drug laws will be here sooner than we think in the name of public safety. Mark my word.

There Are few Scientific Studies Linking Drug Use with Driving Impairment

As mentioned above, currently, no drug per se laws exist.

In addition, there are very few studies, if any, that show that a person that has a specific amount of a given drug in their blood, will impair their ability to drive a car.

When a person consumes a drug, their body breaks the drug down and the person's liver metabolizes it and metabolites are created.

There are no scientific studies that show that a person that has X amount of metabolites in their blood stream is too impaired to drive a car. A second problem is that with many drugs, including marijuana, metabolites can remain in a person's body for a month or longer. Thirdly, what else can create a specific metabolite?

If law enforcement analyzes a blood sample long enough, they're going to find something.

If a certain metabolite that points to a certain substance is found, law enforcement is going to say, using their pseudoscience and their "criminalists" of course: "*metabolite X is in the blood sample, and metabolite X points to drug Y, so therefore the person has taken drug Y and is too impaired to drive a car safely.* "That will be the government's argument.

Because Drug Metabolites Can remain in a Person's System for a Protracted Length of Time, It Can Be Difficult to Prove When Impaired Actually Exists

Because a metabolite is in a person's blood does not mean that the person is too impaired to drive a car safely.

In the United States, an accused person is innocent unless the person is proven guilty with reliable evidence beyond reasonable doubt.

Basically there are forces out there that would like to force accused persons to prove their innocence. This is not the American way.

Interviewer: A person could have smoked marijuana 10 days ago and be sober for the past nine days, and the government will still try to get the person convicted.

Manuel Barba: This is absolutely true, because all substances break down in the human body and metabolize into other substances before exiting the body. Moreover, remnants of any given substance can remain in the body for weeks, or months.

For example, marijuana metabolites can remain in the human body for 90 days or more, and will show in a blood test, but certainly the person is not impaired just because the metabolite is present in the blood.

Which Drugs Are Most Frequently Attributed to Drug-Related DUIs?

Interviewer: What are the most common drugs that people are being charged with DUI for? Can you list both prescription and illegal?

Manuel Barba: Well, Marijuana is common. There are a large number of people that smoke marijuana. Colorado and the state of Washington have legalized it. It's just crazy that there's this war on drugs and making this substance illegal when it's probably no worse than alcohol.

Sleeping and Anti-Anxiety Drugs Are Frequently Attributed to DUIs as Well as Marijuana, Although the Current Climate Is for Prosecuting Drivers Taking Prescription Medications

In addition to Marijuana, other common drugs that are frequently attributed to DUIs are Ambien and other sleeping medications; anxiety drugs such as Xanax, Zoloft, or Soma would also be included in this category.

Today, the big push is not the illegal drugs, but for prescription drugs.

Again, this is because the government has learned that they can make a lot of money on DUIs by arresting and convicting people for DUI. So the government is getting creative and thinking of more ways to convict people for having some substance in their system, and then putting forth the position that the person is too impaired to safely drive a car as a result of the substance. It's a new source of income. DUI really has become a funding mechanism for law enforcement.

Hiring an Attorney to Defend a DUI Charge Allows for the Possibility of the Charge being Reduced or Dismissed and the Penalties Mitigated

Interviewer: Speaking in approximates, what level of success have you had in either getting charges reduced or fines or jail time or other punishments mitigated?

Manuel Barba: I have had great success. What I tell people when they ask me that question is this—every case is different and all factors must be analyzed because until this is done, we really don't know the specifics of a given case. What happens in one DUI case has nothing to do with another DUI case. The only thing that DUI cases may have in common is that they are charged as a DUI.

In reality, we are NOT dealing with apples to apples. With DUI cases, some are apples, some are oranges, and some are pineapples and plums. The facts and the evidence in each case are different, thus raising different issues. Sure there are similarities, but there are great differences too.

Because of the foregoing, it is impossible to put a percentage on the success of any given case.

If a lawyer gives a prospective client a percentage of success at a first meeting, the lawyer is telling the prospective client something that they may want to hear to get hired. Any lawyer that knows what he is doing knows that is not accurate information.

I have handled thousands of DUI cases, and have had many cases reduced from a DUI to a reckless driving or to a reckless driving with alcohol. I have had cases reduced to not using a turn signal or failing to observe a traffic sign. I have had cases dismissed outright in the pretrial stage or after winning a suppression motion.

I have had many cases where the jury found my client not guilty of DUI after a trial. The point is, it is very difficult to put a "percentage" on the outcome of any given case, because each case has different issues, and it really depends on what those issues are.

Are DUI cases complex? Yes, very much so. Are they defensible cases? Yes, they absolutely are. But without completely analyzing a case, it is impossible to know the issues and the defenses of that case.

Does California Allow Alternate Punishments for DUI Convictions?

Interviewer: Are there alternative punishments or diversion programs for first time DUI offenders, such as home detention, ankle bracelets, and community service?

Manuel Barba: The normal term of diversion means that if the accused person completes a class successfully, etc., the criminal case will get dismissed.

In California, there is no diversion in that sense for a person accused of DUI.

Now that's not to say that a DUI case cannot get dismissed, or reduced to a lesser charge – this is the goal in defending every DUI case. But it depends on the problems found when analyzing the case. The more problems we can find, the more negotiating power we have. A good prosecutor will recognize valid problems with the evidence and negotiate for a good resolution to resolve a DUI case.

In Some Cases, You May Serve Your Jail Time through Electronic at-Home Monitoring

If a person is convicted of a DUI, many courts require jail time.

A first misdemeanor DUI conviction is punishable by up to 6 months in jail; a second misdemeanor DUI, with a prior within 10 years, is punishable from 96 hours in jail up to 1 year in jail. A third misdemeanor DUI, having two priors within 10 years, is punishable by a minimum of 120 days in jail with a maximum of 1 year in jail.

Upon a conviction, jail can be served in different ways. For instance, there are weekend work release programs where the convicted person can be assigned to a work location usually at a county facility. Instead of jail, a person can be assigned to clean up parks or pick up trash on the freeway. The person gets to go home at the end of the day.

Community service may also be an option instead of jail. A person may be assigned to a church or some other nonprofit organization to complete the assigned jail time. The person also gets to go home at the end of the day.

A person can also serve their jail time by electronic home confinement, if available. This option allows the person to go to their normal job each day, however, the person must return home by the scheduled time. It is like being grounded.

The availability of the different programs depends on what court your case is in and what county.

Remember these programs, if available, are in lieu of the required jail time. However some courts require the actual jail time or at least a part of it, with the remainder served in one of the programs.

The Courts Have the Discretion Not to Impose Jail for a First DUI Offense

It really depends on what jurisdiction and what court the case is in. Some courts don't require jail on a first time DUI, some courts do. It also depends on the prosecutor and how harsh they want to be.

Can a DUI Be Raised from a Misdemeanor to a Felony Charge?

Interviewer: What factors will enhance or aggravate a DUI charge? Can a DUI be raised to a felony charge?

Some Circumstances Are Wobblers—the DUI Could Be Filed as a Misdemeanor or a Felony

Manuel Barba: If a person was arrested for DUI and was involved in an auto accident and someone was injured, the prosecutor can file charges alleging DUI causing bodily injury (VC23153). This charge is known as a "wobbler," which means that the charge could be filed as a misdemeanor or a felony.

In addition, if a person is arrested for a DUI and has three prior convictions within 10 years, the new DUI can also be charged as a felony or a misdemeanor. Most of the prosecutors in the jurisdictions that I work will charge it as a felony because they want to punish people the most that they can.

Also, if a person is arrested for a DUI and has a prior felony DUI conviction (within 10 years), the new DUI will be charged as a felony.

If a person was arrested for DUI and was involved in an auto accident and someone was killed, felony charges will also be filed.

When my office conducts its investigation, we want to know all of the facts relating to the DUI arrest. What led to the initial stop or contact? Does the person have any prior DUI arrests and/or convictions? Was there an auto accident? Was anyone injured? What was the extent of any injury? Keep in mind, it doesn't have to be a serious injury; a scratch on the forehead, etc. is enough for a felony charge to be filed.

Are the DUI Laws Different for a Commercial Driver?

Interviewer: How do DUI laws differ for drivers that have a commercial driver license?

Manuel Barba: In California, DUI laws differ for drivers with commercial driver licenses (i.e., Class A or B) that are arrested for DUI; the consequences from the Department of Motor Vehicles (DMV) differ as well.

Commercial License Driver in Non-Commercial Vehicle: For instance, if a driver that is arrested for a regular DUI (VC23152 (a)(b)(e)) while driving their personal car, and just happens to have a commercial driver license, the court case will be treated the same, meaning the commercial license will have no bearing on the court case.

HOWEVER, the DMV Administrative Per Se (APS) hearing consequences will differ in that if the driver with a commercial license loses the DMV APS hearing (see pages 49-54) or fails to request a hearing within the 10 days, the DMV will suspend the *commercial* driver license for 1 year on a first time DUI (suspension is for 3 years if a hazardous materials transport certificate).

Although the commercial license will be suspended for 1 year, the driver is eligible to convert their driver license to a normal class C license after the first 30 days and get a restricted license. However, if the driver does convert to the class C license, the driver will have to re-apply for the commercial license after the 1 year commercial license suspension ends. If the driver does not convert to the class C license, the driver will be eligible to have the commercial license reinstated after the 1 year suspension.

If the driver gets a *second* DUI within the 10 year priorability period, the commercial license will be revoked for life.

Commercial License Driver in Commercial Vehicle: The *per se* blood alcohol concentration level (BAC) for a driver with a commercial license driving a commercial vehicle is 0.04% (VC23152(d) and VC 23153(d)); thus if a driver with a commercial driver license is driving a commercial vehicle with a BAC of 0.04% or more, the commercial driver can be arrested and convicted of DUI. This lower BAC level is based on federal regulations; this offense is a misdemeanor, punishable like any other violation of §23152 or 23153 of the Vehicle Code.

Again, the DMV Administrative Per Se (APS) hearing consequences for a commercial driver licenseare a 1 year suspension on a first time DUI (suspension is for 3 years if a hazardous materials transport certificate), and a life time revocation on a second DUI within 10 years.

Additional Adminsitrative Consequence: In addition, a commercial driver can *administratively* be ordered out of service for 24 hours if the driver is found to have a BAC of 0.01% or more (Title 13, Cal. Code of Regs. §1213.1 (c)(d)(e) and (f)). Violation of this administrative regulation is an infraction (CVC §34506.3) which is punishable by a fine. Thus, not only is it an infraction offense to operate a commercial vehicle with a BAC of 0.01% or more, it isalso an infraction offense to operate the commercial vehicle for the next 24 hours once the out-of-service order was issued.

DUI laws relating to drivers with commercial driver licenses and endorsements/certificates are complicated, therefore the commercial driver should consult an expert DUI defense attorney.

DUIs and Persons Holding Professional Licenses

Interviewer: How does a DUI affect a person who holds a professional license, like a Doctor or Lawyer?

Manuel Barba: An arrest and/or conviction for DUI may bring consequences from the California licensing agencies which govern the driver's professional license.

For example, EMTs/Paramedics are governed by the California Emergency Medical Authority; Nurses are governed by the California Board of Registered Nursing; Lawyers are governed by the California State Bar; and Doctors are governed by the Medical Board of California.

The reporting requirements as well as the extent of the consequences for a DUI arrest and/or conviction will vary depending on the particular licensing agency.

If a person holding a professional license is arrested for DUI, it is in their best interest to hire an expert DUI defense attorney to defend them in the DUI case in order to protect the professional license.

What is the Best Way to Recover from a DUI Charge?

Interviewer: What have you seen people do once their case is over or even ongoing, to get back on their feet and live a normal life as fast as possible?

Your Best Strategy Is to Hire an Attorney that is an Expert in DUI Defense

Manuel Barba: I think the best strategy is to hire an expert DUI lawyer that's going to handle the case for you with confidence. What I tell a client is: "let me worry about the case now" so that the client can go on with their daily life.

Now the above advice obviously depends on the seriousness of the case. If the case is a felony, the client must be in court for each court hearing but worrying about the case isn't going to make it any better.

I've had clients say: "Well, I had a vacation I was planning, should I go?" In most cases I tell the client to move forward with their life as they normally would. It is going to take my office time to gather all of the evidence and complete the necessary analysis, etc. so that we know what we are up against, and to determine how to best defend the case.

Let Your Attorney Do His or Her Job and Try to Resume Your Normal Activities

A client can sit home and worry, or they can get on with their life and let us do our job. It is best for the client to go on with their life and live just like they normally would, day-to-day.

Of course we check in with our clients from time to time so they have updates regarding their case. I have a *client liaison* on staff, and his job is primarily to work with our clients and keep them informed.

I am in court almost every day, so if a client has a question about their case, their contact is our client liaison. My client liaison is there in the office every day to get our clients the information that they need. My client liaison can email or text me as needed if there is an urgent issue.

Customer service is important to me and having good communication with our clients is essential, so that our clients can get on with their life without worry.

DUI Defense Case History

Interviewer: Please share with us your favorite victory in defending a DUI case.

Manuel Barba: I have a number of victories, but probably my favorite was a client that allegedly had a BAC of 0.24%from a breath test. After investigating and analyzing the case, clearly I knew he wasn't truly a 0.24% BAC based on what he had told me he had to drink, but more importantly based on the arresting officer's observations of my client.

My client had just finished having 3 drinks before he got stopped by the cop for not using his turn signal.

Can Issues with the Breathalyzer Result in Inaccurate Readings?

The trial was really all about the reliability of the breath test results. The jury found my client not guilty despite the alleged 0.24% BAC.

The prosecutor that was handling the case would not listen when I tried to settle the case before trial. I remember when we were going to trial, the prosecutor was so arrogant. She had this attitude like: "why are you bothering to take this case to trial?"

I have a saying: "I like to teach prosecutors about DUI cases one trial at a time. "The smugness fell off the prosecutor's face when the jury came back with a not guilty verdict; she was floored. All of a sudden her attitude changed and now she blamed the jury for this miscarriage of justice.

No, the jury got it right because the jury listened to the evidence. Using our expert witnesses, I was able to teach the jury about the problem with the breath test in this case; it was not employed properly as my client was still absorbing the alcohol, and as a result, the breath test machine was overstating the results.

The evidence showed that my client had just finished drinking 3 drinks 20 minutes before he was stopped by the cop, who had literally followed him out of the bar parking lot. My client had eaten dinner about 45 minutes before.

The cop's observations were that he smelled an odor of alcohol and that my client had "slow speech" and that his eyes were red. My client had NO unsteady gait and performed well on the field sobriety tests.

First of all, odor of alcohol means nothing more than recent drinking, which is not illegal. Red eyes could mean someone is impaired, but it can also mean that someone is tired (it was 2 a.m.), or has allergies. "Slow speech" is not slurred speech, and considering that the officer had never talked to my client before he had no idea what his normal speech sounded like.

No unsteady gait? Good performance on the field sobriety tests? And they are alleging my client had a 0.24% BAC? Really? That's absurd. Think about it: someone who has a BAC of 0.24%, which is 3 times over the legal limit, should be falling down drunk.

The government's "criminalist" had testified that all persons are too impaired to safely drive a car at a BAC of 0.08%. On cross examination, I asked the criminalist: "so at a 0.08% BAC a person would have mental impairment? YES. Physical impairment? YES. So at a 0.15% BAC a person should be impaired even more than at a 0.08%? OH YES! So at a 0.24% BAC a person should be visibly impaired? OH YES! That's a lot of alcohol to have in one's system? OH YES! At a 0.24% a person would be falling down drunk? OH YES!

The reality was my client was not falling down drunk, in fact, he walked normal (having no unsteady gait), he had no slurred speech, and he performed well on the field sobriety tests.

The opinion of our forensic toxicologist at trial was that my client had a BAC of 0.04% to 0.06% at the time of driving. The opinion was based on the evidence that showed my client ate dinner 45 minutes before the stop, and then drank 3 drinks finishing 20 minutes before the stop. The absorption rate of the alcohol would have been greatly reduced due to the food in the stomach.

A BAC of 0.04% to 0.06% was consistent with my client's good performance on the field sobriety tests, having no unsteady gait, and not being impaired. The jury agreed, and the case was over.

That's probably my favorite case. But I have had other cases with similar situations and outcomes.

Interviewer: Now that someone has read this book and they're convinced that they should call your office for a consultation, what's the best way to get a hold of you?

Manuel Barba: Well, the best way to get in contact with me is to call my office: (866) 442-2722 or (951) 680-9125 or (760) 770-3377. My staff that answers the phones will get the callers' information and set them up for an appointment to come see me.

Using email is not always good to contact me because I get literally hundreds of emails in a day as I am a member of a number of LISTSERVES from various scientific organizations, legal organizations, etc. Plus, I'm in court almost every day so I may not see my emails until the next day, depending on how much time I have.

My office staff is always available. They're here to serve my clients and that's the easiest way to get in contact with me.

DISCLAIMER

This publication is informational only. No legal advice is being given, and reading this material creates no attorney-client relationship. If you are facing legal issues, whether criminal or civil, seek professional legal counsel to have your questions answered.

Law Office of Manuel J. Barba
3800 Orange Street, Suite 100
Riverside, CA 92501
(866) 442-2722 | (951) 680-9125 | (760) 770-3377

www.BarbaLawyer.com
www.aggressiveDUIdefense.com
www.PalmSpringsDUI.com

Made in the USA
Monee, IL
04 November 2026

67385036R00066